Well-Versed Dogs

Well-Versed Dogs

LANCE PERCIVAL
ILLUSTRATED BY LALLA WARD

W.H. ALLEN · LONDON
1985

Printed and bound in Great Britain by
Mackays of Chatham Ltd, Kent
for the Publishers, W.H. Allen & Co. PLC
44 Hill Street, London W1X 8LB

ISBN 0 491 03710 4

For Serena

Contents

Well-Versed Dogs

Whether you love dogs or hate them
These verses are easy to figure;
Not *very* well versed, but even the worst
Will trigger a risible snigger.

Look up the verse on your favourite dog
And decide if you could do better.
If so, don't pretend, straight away send
The author a very rude letter.

Harrier

Till recently the Harrier was not a well-known name,
Then it changed its lifestyle and came back into fame.
Harriers used to hunt in packs, chasing after hare;
Now they take off vertically – straight up in the air.

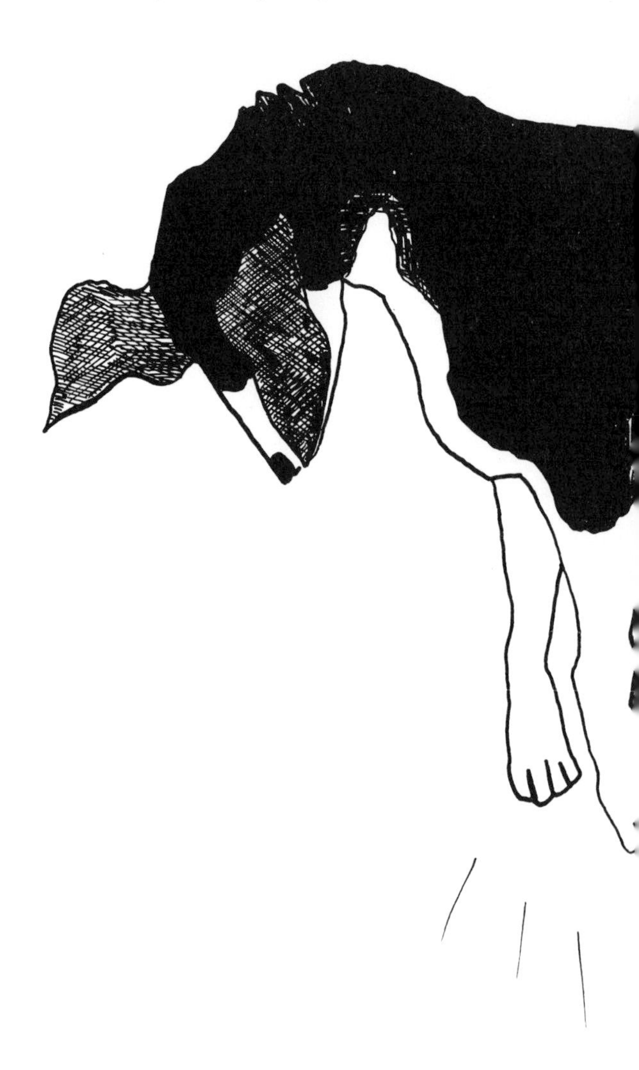

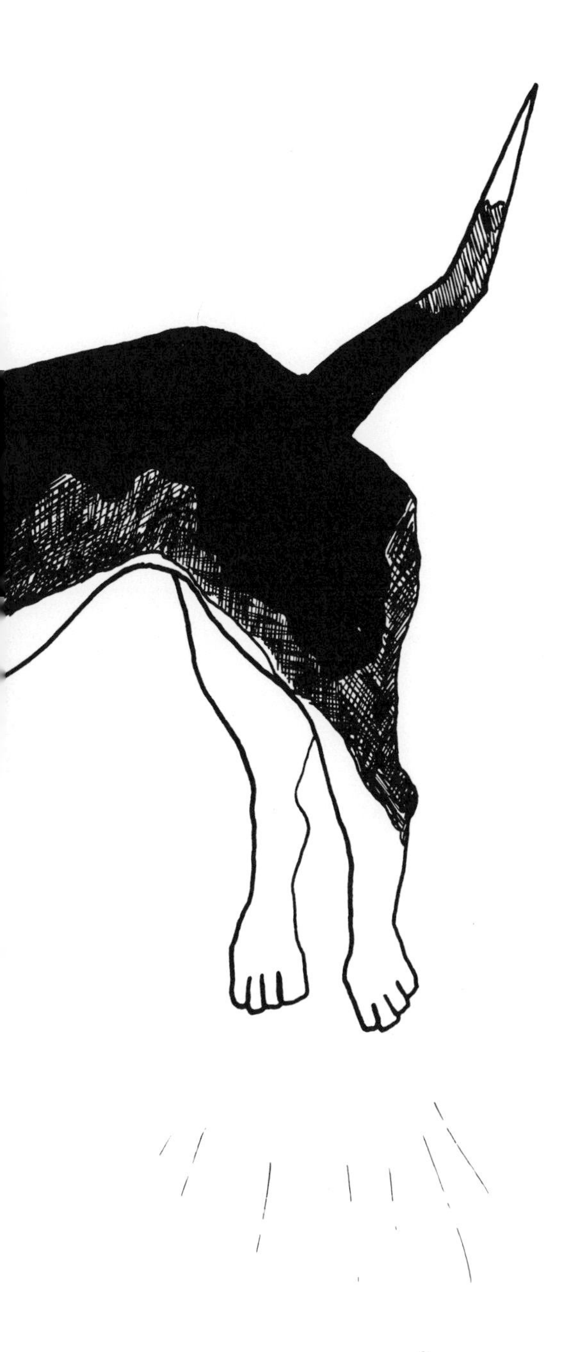

Angus The West Highland Terrier

Angus the West Highland Terrier
Very seldom attacks,
But och he detests any human pests
That call themselves Sassenachs.

He was told as a bairn he was bred from a Cairn,
Pure Scot with a coat pure white.
So imagine the shock, when Angus, a Jock,
Was sent to the Isle of Wight.

The dogs of Ryde have nae sense of pride
When hearing a piper's lilt.
At times he'd die for some haggis pie –
Or even a sniff up a kilt.

No, the Isle of Wight is not worth a light
If you're a Celtic supporter.
So Angus was grim – it was too far to swim
Across the Solent water.

His Master showed Angus 'The Needles',
But they dinne compare, you know,
With Terrier rambles, chasing Campbells
All the way down Glencoe.

Cowes is the port where Angus paid court
To a plain bitch mongrel called Cherry.
She had a weird pong, but she did belong
To the man who captained the ferry.

So he hitched a ride to the other side
And gave Cherry some goodbye licks,
But as he can't drive, he walked the M5 –
And is now halfway up the M6.

One Black Dog

In A2-23 at a dogs' home
Lay a puppy alone and agog,
Who of course wasn't able to see the cage label
Which simply read, 'One Black Dog'.

He vaguely remembered his owners,
But mostly the last episode
When they took him quite far, for a drive in their car
And then dumped him out on the road.

When found he was practically starving,
Whining and oh so frail;
But they patched him OK, listed him 'stray',
And then put him up for sale.

The barking and howling of three hundred dogs
Scared him to such a degree
That he shivered all day, lying down in the tray
Of Kennel A2-23.

In the daytime shadows would cross his face
And he'd look up to face human stares.
He heard them surmise, 'H'mm, quite like his eyes,
But I don't think much of his ears.'

The dog next door said, 'Better buck up –
If you want to find a new owner,'
But he didn't find any joy from mankind,
And preferred to just be a loner.

Two weeks went by, no offer to buy,
The other dogs had more luck.
Till one bright day, he was feeling OK,
When suddenly – kennel cough struck.

Kennel cough, on the whole, is kept under control,
But a virus like wildfire spread;
The vets did their best, but he'd lost life's zest,
Next day 'One Black Dog' was dead.

It's a dog's life they say – who cares anyway?
So to you a moral I'll flog:
If you cannot spare some patience and care –
For God's sake don't get a dog.

Shih Tzu

A Shih tzu is the lion dog of Tibet and China fame.
A Shih tzu bears the great traditions of the Buddhist flame.
A Shih tzu is a breed to be admired, but all the same
A Shih tzu on the pavement outside my house, lived up to its name.

Winston The Bulldog

Winston is a Bulldog
He's British through and through;
When you think of 'Rule Britannia'
You think of Bulldogs too.

Winston goes to sleep each night
Wrapped in the Union Jack;
And when he hears 'God Save the Queen'
He stands with a rigid back.

He represents Great Britain,
Her might and power and will;
That's why, right now, poor Winston
Is looking rather ill.

For Britain's just an island now,
Twenty miles from the Frogs;
So Winston's gone to the vet, I'm afraid,
And Britain's gone to the dogs.

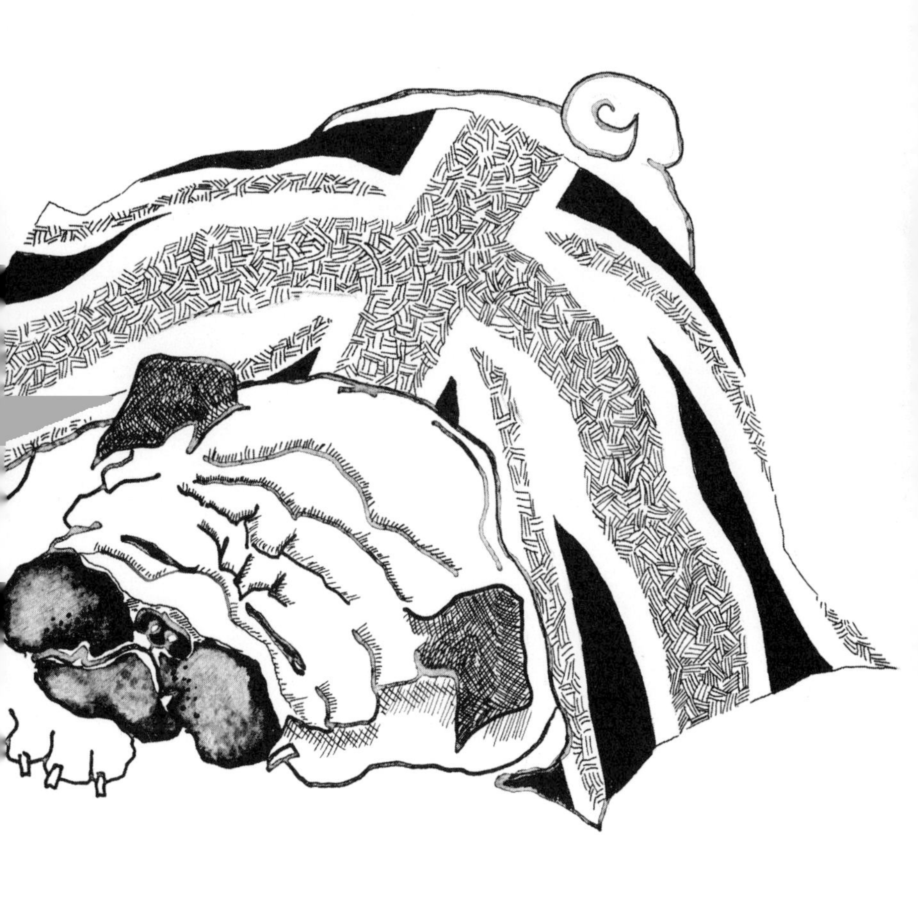

Asoki The Akita

Asoki the Akita is loved by everyone
Who's a native of Japan, the land of Rising Sun.
So you'll find inside her kennel, in downtown Tokyo,
A Sony television and Toshiba video.

A Panasonic musicmaster may sound rather fishy,
But she's also got a tumble dryer out of Mitsubishi.
A Datsun car, a Yamaha, it really makes you sick –
British dogs are lucky if they've got a bone to pick!

KEEP OUT

Dai The Welsh Corgi

Dai was a plain Welsh Corgi,
As common as muck he'd been
Till he learnt with elation some distant relation
Was a household pet to the Queen.

Dai read, in a dog-eared tabloid
That his cousin 'snapped like a chimp'
Which was borne out when *Kennel News at Ten*
Showed the Queen going round with a limp.

Dai was fed up with saying iechyd Da,
Which didn't mean he was disloyal;
He loved the Welsh valleys and the back alleys
But thought that he ought to be Royal.

So whenever Dai saw human legs
He would nip them right in the bud;
It was not out of spite, but to see if they might
Possess any true blue blood.

When Prince Charles came to Carmarthen,
Dai nipped over there with respect,
But he heard Charles say, 'Take that Corgi away',
Or words to that effect!

So Dai rushed over to Princess Di
And performed his only trick:
With amazing knack, he rolled on his back,
And then gave her tootsies a lick.

Nowadays Dai is called David,
As a dog he's one in a million;
He sits all alone on a Corgi throne
As personal guard to Prince William.

Groverbridge The Greyhound

Groverbridge the Greyhound can go at a hell of a pace,
And you should know that while a pro he never lost a race;
His racing days are over, but he now lives near a park
And sprints along the football pitch daily for a lark.

One day, to his amazement, on his morning stroll,
He found an Old English Sheepdog, lying down in goal.
Groverbridge crouched down and thought, 'The silly bitch,
I'll show her who is champion,' and raced off up the pitch.

He went off like a bullet, past the half way line –
Penalty area coming up – Groverbridge is fine.
He knew he was alone, so he wasn't backward looking,
When suddenly, that 'silly bitch', the sheepdog, overtook him.

Groverbridge was so ashamed at losing to a bitch,
He told the sheepdog, 'Ok, smartass – race back down the
pitch.'
Groverbridge tore away, he looked like doing the ton,
But right on the goal line the English Sheepdog *won.*

Did she have a turbo engine helping her to cheat?
Did she have a double whom he somehow didn't meet?
He couldn't comprehend his loss of Greyhound glory,
But of course he'd never heard of a Shaggy Sheepdog Story!

Muffin The Lhasa Apso

Muffin the Lhasa Apso is never in a hurry
And he's never seen Tibet as he lives in Esher, Surrey.
He knows he's rather small, but he gives a mighty yap
If any busybody tries to put him on their lap.

He's sturdy, he's courageous, to be absolutely fair,
His coat is quite magnificent with all that lengthy hair;
But there's *so* much round his face, to be absolutely blunt,
I'm never really sure which is back and which is front.

Scruff The Mongrel

Part Terrier, Spaniel, Collie and Hound
Is the mongrel make-up of Scruff;
He has a nice home, but prefers to roam
Out in the rain living rough.

He'll climb through a hedge, wade in a ditch
And then roll in revolting stuff;
From a mile away, other dogs say,
They can smell the arrival of Scruff.

Under some brambles he'll tear his coat,
But I think he's especially fond
Of rolling in mud, chewing the cud
And a swim in a stagnant pond.

When filthy dirty and soaking too
He tires of being a Rover:
Prepare for doom, as he enters the room,
And *then* shakes himself all over.

On to your sofa, carpet, and walls,
Bits of muck will be hurled;
But don't be appalled, that's why he's called
The scruffiest dog in the world.

Pete And Penny The Lovers

Pete and Penny are two nice dogs
Who live on adjoining farms;
But when they announced they'd fallen in love
The country was up in arms.

'Penny, of course, is far too young.'
'Pete's manners are very slack.'
'What's a dog who is mostly white,
Doing out with a bitch who's black?'

'Their breeds are completely different,
So we can't allow this affair.'
'The one thing that we don't require
Is mongrel puppies round here.'

And yet, so far, oddly enough,
No one has tried to advise
Pete and Penny about one thing,
And that is their problem of size.

Their problem of size is enormous.
Oh, perhaps I forgot to explain:
Pete is a tiny Chihuahua
And Penny's a Great Big Dane!

The Irish Setter

The Irish Setter's a lovely chestnut red
But also it's a teeny bit thick in the head.
There are lots of books
On their lovely looks,
So you may even want to cock some snooks,
But I still say, they're all a bit thick in the head.

If you don't believe me, take one out to play.
Let it off the lead to run away.
You won't see it again,
And I should explain,
All your efforts will be in vain,
Even though you call its name all day.

There's a Gordon and also an English Setter,
Both of which in every way are better.
So choose and buy,
Don't ask me why,
But there's one thing that I can't deny,
I'm still in love with the Loony Irish Setter.

Patch

Patch is a mixture of various breeds,
Not that he really cares why;
He knows that his name very simply came
From his white patch over one eye.

The rest of his coat is more or less black,
And his pet joy in life is to scratch –
Not, if you please, to eradicate fleas,
But simply to have a good scratch.

His chat-up style with lady dogs
The better breeds can't match.
There's no doubt that at woofy chat –
There ain't a patch on Patch.

The trouble is, when he starts to chat,
The lady dogs all sit down –
Because Patch you see, doesn't know that he
Has the *coldest* nose in town!

Wendy The Labrador

Wendy is a Labrador, whose joy is sniffing grass.
Not the stuff in fields and parks, I'm talking about *grass*.
Wendy's a police dog and she's finely trained to know
If there's drugs in any luggage which has landed at Heathrow.

Don't ask me how she does it, but Wendy is the bane
Of marijuana smugglers (and heroin or cocaine).
She works *below* the terminal, so no one knows at all,
Why people are arrested quickly in the customs hall.

Other dogs ignore her and it's rather curious why...
It's not that she is snobbish, they think she's rather 'high'.
They think she's got a one-track mind with very little scope,
But one thing is for certain, Wendy's not a *dope*.

If you are a smuggler, you're bound to wonder whether
Wendy sniffs out plastic luggage better than real leather.
Either way, I fancy, that your odds are rather bleak,
Cause she will be the witness when your... *case* comes up next week.

Perky The Pointer

Perky the Pointer had one great fault –
It was not that he was disjointed –
But his crying shame, when it came to game,
Was he simply wasn't appointed.

It wasn't entirely pointless
For Perky to join in a hunt,
But sad to say he noticed one day
That his point had gone very blunt.

A Pointer's nose, body and tail
Should point in one straight line.
But Perky's absurd – when he saw a bird,
He sat down and let out a whine.

As the bird flew high, away in the sky,
He wagged his tail like a pup.
His master went spare, saying, 'Perky, look here,
It's time that you sharpened up.'

So Perky found an old mirror,
Which was lying behind a hedge,
He felt such an ass, when he looked in the glass,
He could see that he'd lost his edge.

So he brushed his coat, straightened his tail,
And looked for a neutral appraiser.
He found a tom cat, who admitted that
He now looked as sharp as a razor.

Perky then practised standing still,
And pointing in all his glory.
His master saw that, and shot the tom cat –
Which is sadly the point of this story.

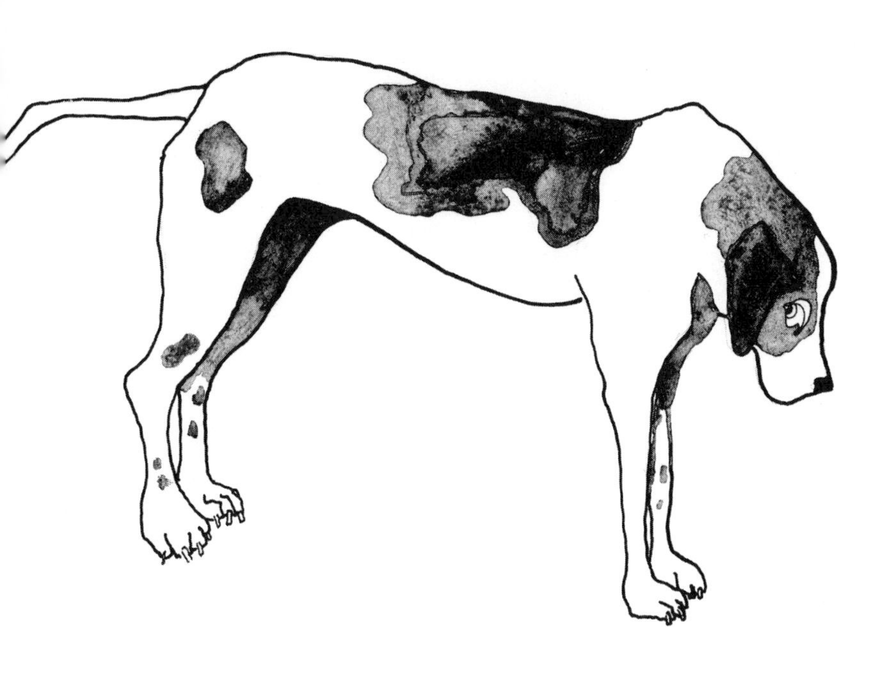

Digby The Doberman

Digby the Doberman Pinscher
Thinks humans are sheer delight,
But whenever he leapt up to people, he kept
Finding they'd freeze out of fright.

His glossy black coat, with rich tan marks,
Was enough to make Digby brag,
But he was deeply shocked, that his tail was docked:
Poor Digby had nothing to wag.

So when the postman came up the path,
Digby could not wag his tail.
The postman would wince and it's two years since
His master received any mail.

He put his front paws round the milkman's neck,
To give him a friendly lick,
And get acquainted – but the milkman fainted,
And since then has been off sick.

His master looks a bit weedy,
But on walks an odd thing would occur:
Wherever he'd go, with Digby in tow,
Other humans would call him 'Sir'.

All the neighbours' homes have been vandalised,
While their owners went out and hob-nobbed.
But Digby's house is as quiet as a mouse
And has never *ever* been robbed.

For Digby you see, yearns to be
A lap dog with bags of charm,
But if ever some boor breaks down the front door,
Digby will take off his arm.

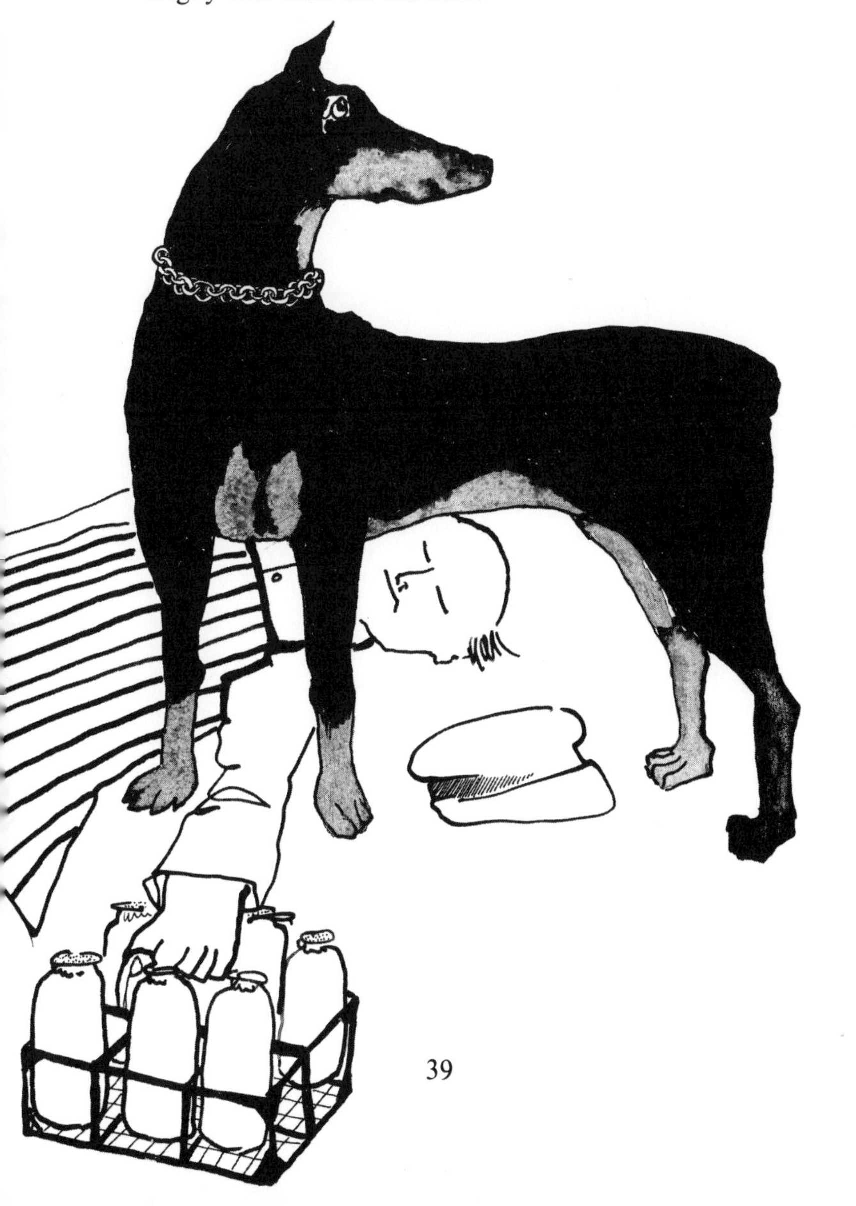

Yin Tong The White Pekinese

Yin Tong's an all-white Pekinese,
Which the average critic insists
Is a snub-nosed race, with a bashed-in face –
And with tootsies prone to cysts.

What is a surprise is in spite of his size
Yin Tong will fight and defy
Boxers, Alsatians, Pugs or Dalmatians...
He's now only got one eye!

So poor Yin Tong sits all day long,
In the flat of a Yorkshire miner;
Filled with memories of when Pekinese
Were the Lion Dogs of China.

They were so refined, as they reclined
In a Mandarin's sleeve looking sleek,
That Confucius say, 'All hills will decay –
When you can't peek at Pekes on the Peak.'

Further back yet, in ancient Tibet,
White Pekes were all part of the drama;
Listening to gongs and old monk's songs,
From the lap of the Dalai Lama.

So a small bed-sit, near a Barnsley pit,
To Yin Tong is frightfully gauche,
'Cause he's awfully posh – well not really posh –
As Pekes pronounce it *pauche*!

Fifi The Toy French Poodle

Fifi the toy French poodle
Can never really explain
Why she's taken for walkies, twelve times a night,
Round the back of the Madeleine.

Fifi knows her mistress is pretty –
Cause whenever they go for a walk
Every single man they pass
Always stops for a talk.

But Fifi reckons there's something about
Her mistress that must be wrong;
Cause although lots of men come back to their flat,
None of them stay very long.

Then one night down by the Opera,
A man touched her mistress' arm,
She said, 'Shall we go?' He replied, 'You should know
You're nicked, cause I'm a gendarme.'

When Fifi reached the gendarmerie,
She had her first canoodle,
As every belle inside the cell
Was accompanied by a male poodle.

Fifi enjoyed that night so much,
She's living in four-leaf clover –
And anytime she wants a good time
She just calls a gendarme over.

Her mistress abandoned her career –
She had to, just to survive.
While Fifi is now (the naughty cow)
A very proud mother of five.

Bertie The Boxer

Bertie the bouncing Boxer affection doesn't lack;
His owners both love Bertie, and Bertie loves them back.
Why do I call him bouncy? Well, I'll tell you about that.
His owners went out working leaving Bertie in their flat.

First he bounced on the sofa and started hell for leather
To rip the cushions open as he loved the feel of feather.
Knocking glasses off the table proved to be diviner;
Then one bound on the dresser wrecked the Dresden China.

He tore up all the carpet that was tacked down to the floor,
Yanked the blankets off the bed and looked around for more.
The cupboard door was open, and as Bertie never quits
He chewed every pair of shoes into tiny little bits.

He knocked a mirror over, then strictly for a laugh
Tore the toilet roll to shreds, and dropped it in the bath.
Chaos and destruction were everywhere to see,
When Bertie heard the turning of the Front Door Key.

He bounced out to the hall – my goodness this was fun –
He hasn't got a tail, so he had to wag his bum.
His owners welcomed Bertie then they had an odd sensation;
Everywhere they looked was total desolation.

They used to have possessions, but they have none anymore –
After Bertie's bouncing, they ended up quite poor.
Of course they punished Bertie, they gave him quite a trouncing
But they never leave him all alone, in case he starts his *bouncing*.

Portuguese Water-Dog

The Portuguese Water-Dog is known for being brave,
And for its hind-quarters that are very closely shaved.
This means its bum is naked, which is why I think it oughta –
Out of a sense of decency – stay sitting in the water!

Hubert The Bloodhound

Hubert is a bloodhound who does one thing very well;
He only needs a whiff to identify a smell.
He's proud of being a bloodhound, but Hubert gets annoyed,
When he's linked with Sherlock Holmes, or even Clement
Freud.

His master likes to entertain a dozen friends or more;
They sit and chat while Hubert lies sprawled across the floor.
But if his nose should rise and twitch, he's the first to know,
That someone in the dining-room has quietly *let one go*.

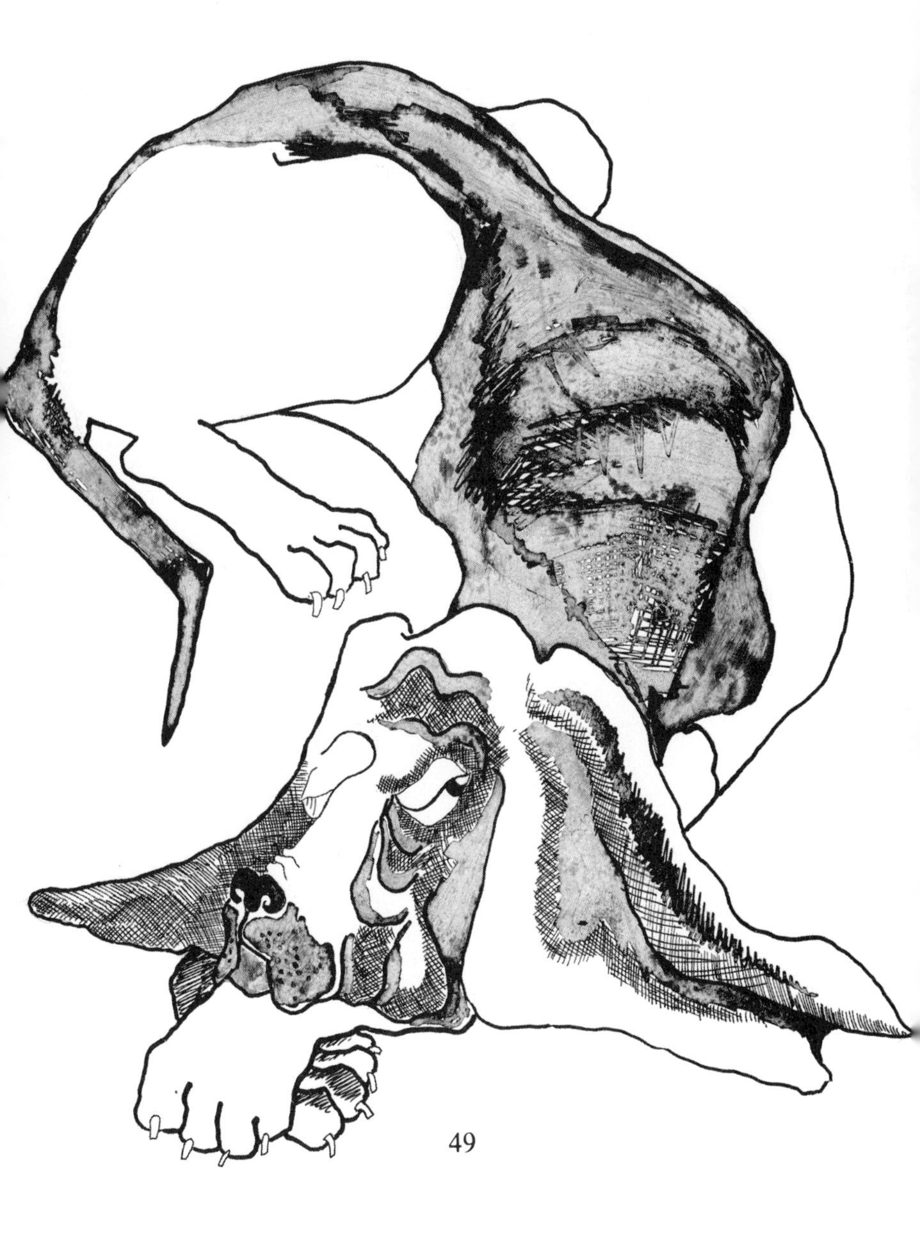

The Owczarek Nizinny

The Owczarek Nizinny
Wants to know who to blame,
For blessing him, on a sudden whim,
With an incomprehensible name.

He's really a Polish sheep-dog,
But impossible to console,
Cause he has to admit, that he's not a Brit,
Which is driving him up the Pole.

He took his name to the Kennel Club,
To see if they would renounce it.
They heard his claim, wrote down his name,
But none of them could pronounce it.

If you meet a tail-less sheepdog,
Who is somewhat shaggy and skinny,
Don't wait all day, just quickly say,
'That's an Owczarek Nizinny!'

Terry The Norwich Terrier

Terry the Norwich Terrier tore up the A 11,
Turned left on the Norwich circular, then on to the A 47.
Next he cut across country, which was really rather naughty,
Zipping down those B roads and back down the A 140.

He whizzed round the cathedral, and out along Thorpe Road,
A blue lamp flashed behind him, but on and on he rode.
Heading towards Great Yarmouth, now he was in a fix,
So he made a right, right again and back up the 146.

Norwich Terriers driving cars? Explain that if you can.
Ah well, Terry's not a dog, he's actually a man.
Terry the Norwich Terrier is the nickname for a sneak
Who goes round nicking cars, and his case comes up next week.

DOG 123 X

Bella The Basset

Bella the Basset has big brown eyes
That look pretty and mournful as well;
But God only knows why he gave her a nose,
Which provides a great sense of smell.

She knows that her coat is lemon-pied
She thinks that the colours improve her.
But all day she's found, nose to the ground,
Picking up scraps like a Hoover.

She knows that her body is long and strong,
While her legs are stocky and short:
This leads to despair, in the open air,
When she's chasing squirrels for sport.

She also knows, from her ancestry,
She was bred for going *under the brush*;
So she has poor views of promoting shoes
That are either called Puppy or Hush

She knows she was born with wrinkles –
She thinks they make her look shrewd.
But being a bit thick, it took years to click
Why her ears dangle down in her food.

Then she noticed her paws tripped over her ears
Whenever she walked along...
And now Bella *knows* why God chose a nose
That is blessed with a great sense of *pong*.

Chinese Crested

I'm afraid the Chinese Crested
In the beauty stakes would flop.
It looks a bit like Surrey,
With a Chinese *Fringe on Top*.

Apart from having a *Leatherhead*
The *Staines* on it's body are thick –
It's hardly *Fleet*, but it's hard to beat
It's miniature *Hampton Wick*.

Rex The King Charles Spaniel

Rex the King Charles Spaniel
Deserved a Royal abode,
But his owner's flat in London was tat
And worse, it was in *Cromwell* Road.

The interior of this Cromwell pit
Was a secret he never divulged.
I don't wish to pry, but I'm sure that's why,
His eyes continually bulged.

He'd walk up to Kensington Gardens
(To avoid Cromwellian malice),
Being rather fond of the Round Pond,
And gazing at Kensington Palace.

Then on to the Albert Memorial
Designed, he thought, by a quack.
The Albert Hall, he did not like at all,
But the dustbins were good round the back.

When he reached his favourite dustbin,
Some mongrel was there on the loose,
Licking her chops, after guzzling the slops
From a carton of orange juice.

Then the mongrel turned, wagged her tail,
And woofed rather coyly, 'I'm Nell.'
Suddenly Rexy felt very sexy,
He adored her commoner's smell.

PURE
ORANGE
JUICE

So he licked her mouth clean, which isn't obscene,
For dogs it's a nice thing to do.
And went on with speed, about how his breed
Were started by King Charles Two.

Nell was impressed, so she asked, 'Do you live
In some palace that's nearby here?'
Rex wouldn't admit to the Cromwell pit,
So he lied, 'In St James' Square...

'Now Nell, for a lark, let's go to the park
Chasing horses along Rotten Row.'
She said, 'I'm not sure your intentions are pure,
Even though you're a Royal, I know.'

Rex vowed she could own his favourite bone,
His collar and far, far more.
She was almost a bride, when right alongside,
Someone opened a big car door.

A man gave a yell, 'Get in the car, Nell.'
So she leapt in the Rolls Corniche.
As she whisked away, Rex was heard to say,
'So much for the *nouveau riche*.'

Arild The Norwegian Elkhound

Arild's the pride of Norway –
Their own Norwegian Elkhound;
But wherever he went, there wasn't the scent
Of a single elk to be found.

That's why he set forth, heading due North,
From the suburbs of Kristiansand.
He got very bored of swimming each Fjord,
And anyway, Elks live inland.

When he reached the Arctic Circle
He began to feel lonely up there,
Cause the only chaps he could find were Lapps
Mucking around with reindeer.

But an elk is an elk, and not the same thing,
Priorities must be in order.
So Arild went on, and on and on,
Till he reached the Russian border.

Elks, of course, are capitalists,
So in Russia they're strictly taboo.
Arild turned round, and next month was found
Looking round Oslo Zoo.

The elks, he was told, were in quarantine –
Some disease which makes them fret;
So he walked overland, back to Kristiansand,
Without seeing an elk ever yet.

When he got home, he was famished,
So he raided the fridge before bed.
No elk to be found, so Arild the Hound
Ate a chocolate *mousse* instead!

Karelian Bear Dog

The Karelian Bear Dog is a breed that's known as Spitz:
A Finnish dog, who's so polite, he never, never spits.
However, when he spots a bear, he gets a little kinky –
Which could be said for lots of people living in Helsinki!

Bernie The St Bernard

High in the Alpine mountains,
Where only St Bernards go,
There's not a sound, as they hunt around,
For lost travellers in the snow.

Bernie was out on patrol one day,
When, after a very steep climb,
He found in a hut, a frozen man, but
Had Bernie got there in time?

Bernie gave him the lick of life,
And a tot from his barrel of brandy,
But the man's dying plea was, 'What will save me
Is a half pint of lemonade shandy.'

Bernie raced home, mixed up the drink,
And brought it back in a tin.
The man hadn't died, but he quietly sighed,
'Is there any chance of a gin?'

So Bernie dragged up a *Gordon's* Setter
To help his cold free-loader,
But the man kept crying, 'I'm simply dying
For a double whisky and soda.'

Vodka, rum and pink champagne...
Bernie thought it had gone too far.
So he brought up some logs, bricks and cement
And together they opened a bar.

Down below in the monastery,
There descended a reverent hush.
Who nicked the drinks? Well the abbot thinks,
That one of his monks is a lush.

Back in the Alps, Bernie has finished
His brandy, so now he hums
A plaintive sound: 'She'll be coming round
The mountain when she comes!'

Penny The Whippet

Penny the Whippet is ever so fast;
She can tear round and round until
The heavens unfold some rain or cold,
Then she always gets a chill.

If you wrap her up in a blanket,
She still won't get enough heat;
She shivers and shakes, trembles and quakes,
And then she refuses to eat.

You can put the central heating on,
Or give the coal fire a try,
But she looks decrepit, barely tepid,
And this is in mid-July.

So you ring the vet for medical help,
And he gives you a useful snippet,
'Got cold in the rain? Oh, not again,
It's always the same with a Whippet!'

Now Penny the Whippet is better,
And rarely affected by rain.
She hasn't improved, but her master's moved
Down to the south of Spain.

So if you ever get a Whippet,
And suddenly down it pours,
Here's some advice, which should suffice,
Quickly *Whip-it* indoors!

Hermann The Rottweiler

If you see a black Rottweiler outside your house one day,
And he answers to the name of Hermann, never, never
say
Things like 'Scram', 'Push off' or 'Get out of it' to Hermann,
Cause he was born in Deutschland and only answers German.

Say, 'Achtung,' he'll stand up straight, rigid to the core.
Shout at him, 'Zieg Heil,' and he'll raise his right front paw.
If you yell, 'Nicht Rauchen,' I'll take an even bet
Hermann will leap up and snatch your lighted cigarette.

'Raus, Raus,' is useful – he'll go straight outside the door.
'Deutschland uber Alles,' and he'll lie down on the floor.
One thing that I beg of you, *never* call him 'Kraut'
Or he'll grab you by the throat and spit little pieces out.

Of course if you speak German, then Hermann is OK,
And to *all* Rottweiler owners I feel I ought to say . . .
I'm sure yours is a darling (in German that is Schätzig)
But I suspect that Hermann is a teeny wee bit Nazi!

Toots The Long-Haired Dachshund

Toots the Long-haired Dachshund
Is long and slung very low;
And although he's bold, he gets very cold
When going for a walk in the snow.

So when it snowed in December,
He didn't know what to do.
He played hide and seek, in the house for a week –
But was *dying* to go to the loo!

Now Toots is normally house-trained,
He'll always go in the garden,
Tread on some flowers, and deliver some showers,
Without even begging your pardon.

He was desperate to go, but not in the snow,
He couldn't have felt forlorner.
He licked a paw in the corridor,
But his back half was still round the corner.

He knew that the floor was sacred,
And that he must *never* mark it;
Which he didn't intend, but round the bend
His rear end was peeing on the carpet.

When his mistress saw it, she screamed,
'That dog will wish it was dead.
I'll give it a hiding,' but Toots was hiding,
Under the attic bed.

The house was searched methodically,
But the hunt for the dog was in vain.
Meanwhile Toots was betting his boots,
That he'd soon have to pee once again!

So he climbed through the velux window,
On to the Welsh tiled roof;
Where Toots was seen, doing the opening scene –
From *Piddler on the Woof*.

Jack The Russell

In a country meadow, I think it's worth reporting,
Lay a couple who were what is really best described as
courting.
When suddenly the girl cried out, 'I'm beyond console –
My mother's favourite earrings have gone down that rabbit
hole.'

The boyfriend rolled his sleeves up and reached down with his
arm,
But when something bit his fingers, he withdrew it with alarm.
And then they saw their saviour, who was flexing every muscle.
A knight in shining armour? No, a dog called Jack the Russell.

They pointed to the rabbit hole, and also to her ears,
And tried to show that earrings usually come in pairs.
So Jack the fearless Russell, went down the rabbit hole
And soon produced four rabbits, three ferrets and a mole.

He was trying to bring a fox out, when suddenly he found,
That halfway up the passage, he couldn't turn around.
So the couple went and borrowed two shovels lying about,
And spent the next three hours digging Jack the Russell out.

They rescued Jack the Russell, but it wasn't till much later,
That they realised they'd created a dirty great big crater.
The farmer sued them both at the local legal hearings –
They were fined a hundred pounds, but they never found the
earrings.

There are two different lessons in this story to be found –
Make sure that your Jack Russell isn't stuck below the ground.
The second's so important that I cannot let it pass –
Never wear your earrings when you're courting in the grass!

Weimaraner

The German Weimaraner is a breed you can't diminish,
It's coloured like a car with metallic silver finish.
Sometimes called the ghost dog, as he looks a trifle spooky,
He's also very handsome – so he gets a lot of nooky!!

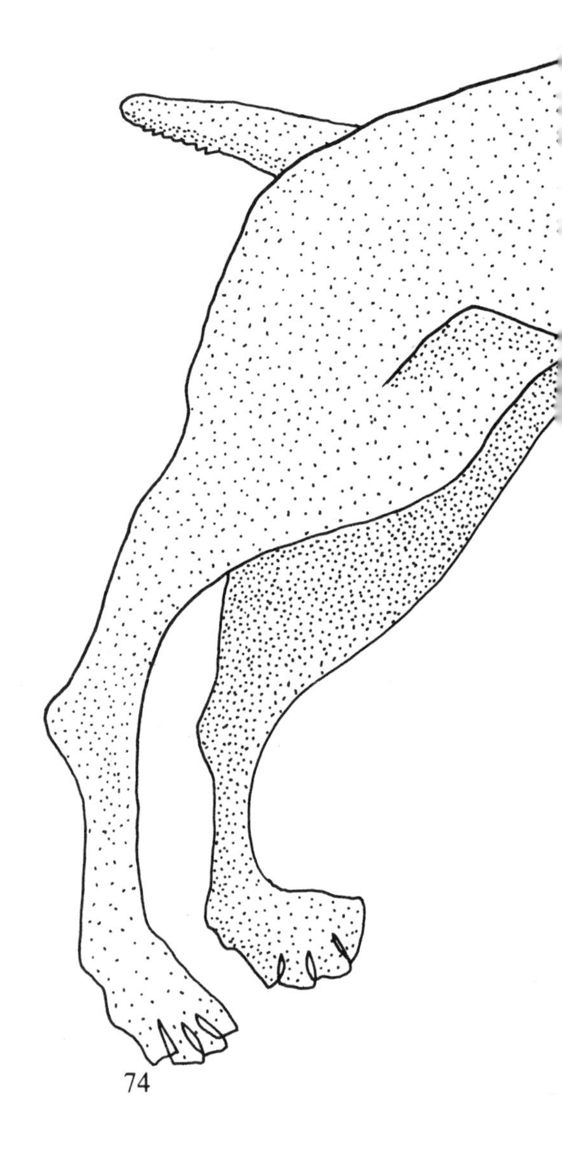

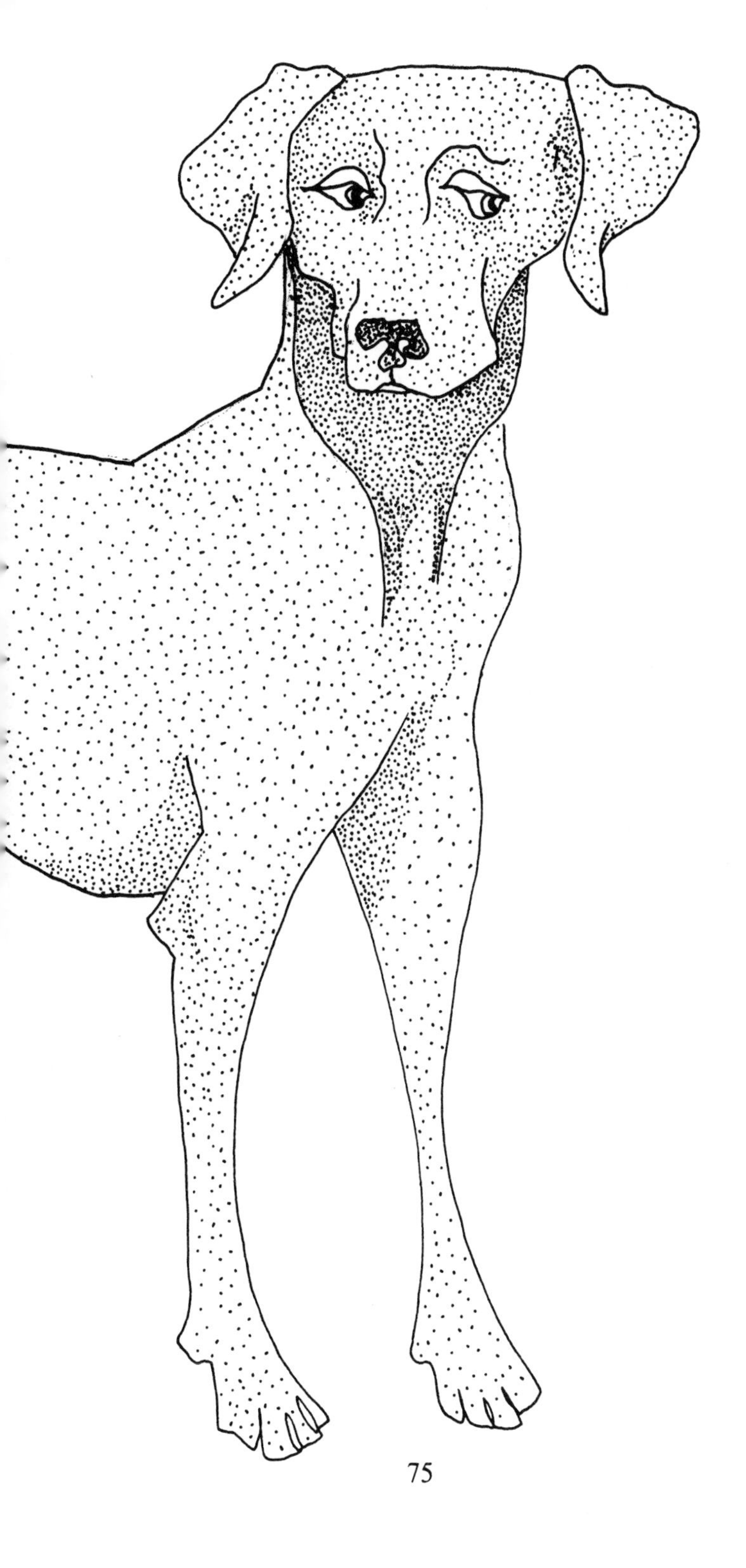

Butch The Beagle

Butch the Beagle's a hound dog, and although he's merry
and bright,
Leave him at home, *he'll* make sure the neighbours are up all
night.
He never comes when you call him, which hardly needs
explaining:
Butch the Beagle's a hound dog, and hound dogs don't like
training.

Take him out for a walk, and he'll simply disappear,
Sniffing round the corn stubs, trying to find a hare.
I asked a Beagle Master, down in Dorset at the time,
If they'd ever caught a hare. He said, 'Yes, in '69.'

But don't tear your hair out, he's a great family pet;
Just because he's obstinate, no need for you to fret.
He's one of the most friendly and most loyal dogs around,
But Butch is still a Beagle, and a Beagle is a hound.

Butch has asked if he can add a P.S. to this verse:-
'Thank you Lance, we Beagles have a grudge that's getting
worse.
We have no real objections to you humans daily choking,
But Beagles as a breed, are strictly *anti*-smoking.'

Sacha The Bull-Terrier

Bull-Terriers are remembered for the one that lived with
Sykes,
But Sacha is a lovely dog, whom everybody likes.
All the same, one little thing, I think you ought to know.
When Bull-Terriers bite, they never let you go.

When a man fell off the pier, Sacha thought that he was
clowning –
By the time he'd surfaced twice, she realised he was drowning.
So she leapt into the ocean and bit his overcoat.
By pulling hard with all her strength, she kept the man afloat.

For this display of gallantry, she won the D.S.O.,
Which is *Doggie's Save in Oceans*, in case you do not know.
She wears it round her collar, the wording's very clear:
'Sacha is the heroine of Brighton's Western Pier.'

So if you're down on Brighton pier, and fall into the sea,
Have no fears, pretty soon, Sacha you will see.
I swear she won't let go, when she grabs your overcoat,
And if you haven't got one, she'll grab you by the throat!

D.S.O

Geoff The Airedale

Geoff the Yorkshire Airedale used to hunt for otter,
But now they've banned the otter, he's an avid
pro-Boycotter.
He thinks that Boycott ought to bat till he's a hundred-and-
one,
As the other Yorkshire batsmen very seldom score a ton.

When Geoff the dog disappears, it means he's gone to see
The idol of his life swing the bat at Headingley.
Two things they have in common . . . they both dislike a duck,
And they both dislike the brass, cause where's there's brass
there's muck.

One day Geoff the Boycott was summoned by committee
And told, 'You are too old,' which seemed a dreadful pity.
Geoff the Airedale sat outside; they thought he'd come to beg.
But when the chairman left the room, he bit him middle-and-
leg!

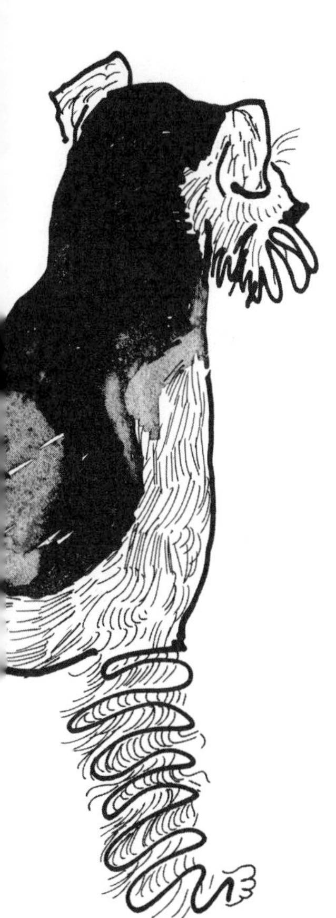

Rod The Rhodesian Ridgeback

Rod the Rhodesian Ridgeback
Had a ridge of hair with the knack
Of growing in reverse, completely inverse
To the rest of the hair on his back.

Rod's a marvellous watchdog,
Put him out at night as a scout –
Through thick and thin, no one gets in
But of course none of you can get out!

He thinks Rhodesian Ridgeback
Has a beautiful African sound;
So he felt very strange when his name was changed
To Zimbabwe Uhare Hound.

Rod the Zimbabwe Uhare Hound,
To him wasn't so appealing;
Which is probably why he declared UDI
In the kennel suburbs of Ealing.

He knows that he's been black-listed,
And he knows he's entirely to blame.
But who's going to attack a Rhodesian Ridgeback?
So Rod has retained his name.

Tuff The Husky

Tuff's a Greenland Husky, who everybody knows
Works all day and half the night for Northern
Eskimos.
But life for Tuff the Husky is no longer what it's been,
Cause everything he used to do, is now done by machine.

Machines can drag great weights about across the slippery
snow.
More machines can work on ice, or even an ice-floe.
When men go hunting far inland, they use a whirly bird –
Life for Tuff the Husky has now become absurd.

They made him go sled-racing, because he was so fast;
Tuff waited till the bets were down, and then he came in last.
He could not stand being used for sport – Tuff was going to pot
Until he read some doggerel verse about a Captain Scott.

Tuff was most impressed; then he heard by *woof of mouth*
That Captain Scott was not up here, but somewhere way down
south.
So he hopped upon an iceberg floating down the deep
Atlantic –
When it melted off Guyana, Tuff was getting frantic.

Then he strolled through South America (very hot and hilly).
Tuff went on until he reached the bottom tip of Chile.
He stowed aboard a weather ship, and then he reached his
goal –
Tuff's the only Husky living near the southern pole.

No machines, no Eskimos, life is really bliss.
In fact if you ask Tuff, only one thing is amiss –
Although he's searched for three whole years, so far he has not
Found a single trace of his hero Captain Scott.

Farouk The Saluki

Farouk the golden Saluki
Was born in the desert sands.
He can hunt gazelle extremely well,
And he loves his Arabian land.

He can spot his prey from far away,
And then he runs like hell,
But he's never content, following a scent:
In the desert there's nothing to smell!

His master is a Bedouin,
And Farouk's joy and pride
Is each night spent, inside the tent,
While the camels sleep outside.

This was an ideal life for Farouk,
Till there was an odd event.
A big oil spray shot up one day,
Right through the floor of the tent.

The Bedouin bought the land before
Anyone else was told.
The initial change, that Farouk found strange,
Was his collar was made of gold.

Then Farouk was flown to London,
To a house in SW1.
Making his mark on a tree in Hyde Park,
Was hardly Arabian fun.

He was feeling sad, when he noticed
A large Islamic dome;
And soon he saw, that there were far more
Arabs here than at home!

So, if you meet a happy Saluki,
With a rich middle eastern bloke;
Use your charm and say 'Salaam'
But don't tell a Kosher joke!

Basenji

Deep in the Congo basin,
Where the jungle grows very dark,
There was found a dog called Basenji,
Who unfortunately can't bark.

It can whisper, chortle or yodel,
Or even laugh for a lark;
But try as it might, all ruddy night,
It cannot emit a bark.

But if you go back three thousand years,
Where the ghost of Egypt looms,
The dogs all look like Basenjis
That are etched on the Pharaohs' tombs.

So next time you see a Basenji,
Remember its long pedigree,
And they're bright as well, cause I've never heard tell
Of one barking up the wrong tree!

Dick The Dalmatian

One Thousand and One Dalmatians, I trust,
Is a film remembered with glee.
Well forget it, as this is the story
Of Number One Thousand and *Three.*

Richard the Third was quite absurd –
As a name it didn't click.
So in view of the marks that were on his coat,
He called himself *Spotted Dick.*

Spotted Dick's idea of fun
Was chasing horses all day,
And as he lived by the Surrey Downs,
He was simply let out to play.

But the name of the Downs was Epsom –
The date first Wednesday in June.
Dick thought, 'There's too many people here
For a mid-week afternoon.'

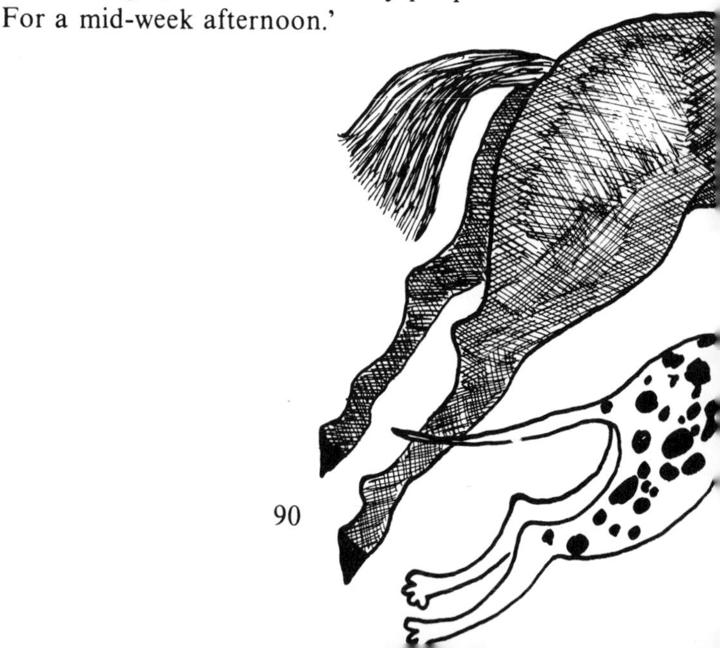

'They're off,' screamed a million humans,
Making Dick feel even forlorner –
Till he suddenly spotted twenty-five nags
Racing round Tattenham Corner.

So Dick leapt out from behind the rails,
And caught up the going rate.
Spotted Dick joined the Derby,
All the way up the home straight.

He ran and ran as fast as he could,
And nearly caused a sensation.
The race was won by a pedigree horse,
By a short head from a Dalmatian.

While the stewards held an inquiry,
Spotted Dick went home to bed.
And his old name's changed from *Richard the Third*
To *Richard the Second* instead.

Claus The German Pinscher

Claus the German Pinscher, out of sense of fun,
Crept up behind his mistress, and *pinsched* her in the bum.
'Claus,' she cried, 'that hurt,' but she didn't even flinch –
She merely cut his food by half – and now *he feels the pinch*!

Rene The Papillon

Rene the toy French Papillon
Knows the real reason why,
His particular breed are indeed
Named after a butterfly.

It's not because his ears stick out
And are fringed with silky hair;
And he cannot fly like a butterfly,
So there's little comparison there.

Rene was shut up when he was a pup,
In the *Diable Chien Pound.*
It was very secure, but Rene was sure
That a means of escape could be found.

He discovered a plank and a barrel,
Which were perfect for what he'd require.
He asked a friend to weigh down one end,
While he sprung over the wire.

But he tripped on the wire going over,
And was upside down as he fell.
They all saw him fly, but he couldn't deny
Being a butterfingers as well.

So the other dogs called him Papillon,
But Rene when asked, will preen,
'It's my Great Escape and not my shape
That was modelled on Steve McQueen.'

Bessie The Alsatian

Bessie is a police dog,
A very well trained Alsatian;
She enjoys her role, on dog patrol,
And is proud of her reputation.

She's nabbed sixteen bank robbers,
Twelve muggers, maybe more;
Shop-lifters two, pick-pockets too,
And burglars by the score.

But there is one type of criminal,
Of whom Bessie can't make sense.
She can easily climb, one bound at a time,
But how do you catch a *Fence*?

Dinger The Golden Retriever

Dinger the Golden Retriever
Has an uncanny knack –
Whatever you try to throw away,
Dinger will bring it back.

If you throw scraps in the dustbin,
With cans and cartons galore,
Dinger will neatly replace it all
In a pile on the kitchen floor.

If you manage to drive a golf ball,
As far as the eye can see,
Dinger will tear down the fairway,
And drop it right back on the tee.

Sling a sweet-paper out of the car
While shooting up the M1,
Dinger will leap out the window,
At any speed up to a ton.

His master works as a teacher,
Which Dinger seems to enjoy.
If ever a pupil runs away,
Dinger retrieves the boy.

Then one day Dinger went for a walk,
To give us a Golden display,
Of how to find yourself when lost –
And he hasn't been seen to this day!

All that's left of Dinger now
Is a snap on the mantelshelf.
You see the problem with Dinger was
He couldn't retrieve himself!

Wellie The Yorkshire Terrier

Wellie's a Yorkshire Terrier,
A titchy sort of a chap;
And as he's afraid of being squashed underfoot,
He's developed a mighty yap.

He can yap and yap so piercingly
That it goes straight through your brain.
But once you've heard him yap you'll never
Tread on Wellie again.

Wellie is short for Wellington,
The Duke and a General too.
He was called that because, when he cocks his leg,
It's a miniature Waterloo.

Yorkies are bred as ratters,
But Wellie's chances are slim;
He gave it up, when he found out,
That the rats were bigger than him!

When his sharp little teeth nip your ankles,
It's his way of saying, 'We're chums.'
And in middle age, when his teeth fall out
He'll suck them to death with his gums.

But the joy of Wellie's titchy size
Is there's many more smells to smell.
His tail's so short when he wags it –
He wags his bottie as well.

Show-dog Yorkies are silver and tan,
With a well groomed silky fluff.
But Wellie's coat is best described
As a blackie-brown mangled scruff.

If you happen to have a baby at home
Who can scream and cry on tap,
Have no fear, it will never compare
With the power of Wellie's yap.

The Four Collies

Of all the names given to dogs,
One is especially tough.
Why are they called Rough Collies?
Rough Collies are far from rough.

Their colourful coats look glorious,
And they're wonderful pets in the home.
All you need is the daily use
Of a good stiff brush and comb.

As for the Border Collie,
No insults may be hurled.
It's passed the test of being the best
Sheepdog in the world.

The Bearded Collie of Scotland
Is covered in shaggy hair;
And wears a beard, to be prepared,
For the freezing cold up there.

If you want an indoor Collie
To fit in the family groove,
The most ideal, with lots of appeal,
Is of course the Collie that's Smooth.

If you get *any* of these four,
I'm sure you'll have some jollies;
Which may not make much sense –
But at least it rhymes with Collies!

Percy The Pug

Percy the Pug looks fierce, but you mustn't be ungracious,
He's nothing to do with pugilists, nor is he
pugnacious.
He seems to have no neck, just a very wrinkled face,
With bulging eyes, which all comprise a permanent grimace.

What Percy's very proud of is his double twisted tail,
And the smoothness of his coat, both in perfect scale.
But there's one thing about Percy, which I do *not* quite adore –
When he breathes, it comes in heaves, snore succeeding snore.

He was very good with kids, till one day a little boy
Took one look at Percy and said, 'Mummy, that's a toy.'
So Percy did a great big belch to scare the little twerp,
Now Percy's place is in disgrace, for letting go one burp.

There's a moral to this story, which I think you should employ,
Pugs look rather miniature, but never call them toy.
If you do, be ready with a portable recorder
And you will find, Pugs don't mind, doing a belch to order.

Duke The Dogue Of Bordeaux

If you haven't met Duke, the Dogue of Bordeaux, you're in
for a big surprise,
He's a Gallic version of Mastiff, and also a massive size.
Duke was born in '82 in the land of the Bordeaux vine,
A very good year for Dogues but lousy for Bordeaux wine.

The Cocker Spaniel

When you see a Cocker Spaniel, call out 'Wotcha Cocker,'
Wotcha's not his name, but that wouldn't shock a
Cocker.
Spaniels aren't all loyal, but the Cocker's never flagging,
Whatever you may say, his tail is always wagging.

When he does something wrong, you may rant and you may
rail,
But the Cocker doesn't mind, he still wags his little tail.
Even if, by chance, you're a Cocker Spaniel knocker,
I'll bet he wags his tail, when you call out 'Wotcha, Cocker.'

Chu Chin The Chow

Chu Chin the Chow is red, but not as *underneath the bed*:
In point of fact he's *very* conservatively bred.
But it's not with Chowy dogma, your mind I'm going to clog,
It's the fact that Chows are very much a one man dog.

When you ring the door bell, Chu Chin starts his howling,
And when you enter you will think that Chu Chin's really
scowling.
That's just his expression, but in one way you are right,
If you offend his owner, you'll get a nasty bite.

Being bitten by a Chow I assure you isn't nice;
So if you hate his owner, here's some good advice:
When you meet him somewhere, walking with his Chow,
Don't say, 'Hello,' turn around and exit, crying, 'Ciao!'

Chesapeake Bay Retriever

Half way down the map of the USA,
You'll discover Chesapeake Bay –
So far, OK.

The dogs there are bound to spring a surprise –
Orangey-yellow eyes
Are an odd disguise.

You don't believe me? Get on a plane today.
You'll find it's a hell of a way
To Chesapeake Bay.

There's nothing more to learn about Chesapeake Bay,
So trust me and stay in the old UK.
OK? OK.

Pip The Miniature Schnauzer

Pip the Miniature Schnauzer was in New York docks one week,
When a Giant Schnauzer jeered at him, calling him 'Pip Squeak'.
Pip said, 'You may be bigger in every single way,
But I'm one of the top ten breeds in *all* the USA.'

The Giant complained, 'It's not our fault, we've all tried very hard
But US Immigration won't give us their green card –
They asked us "What does Schnauzer mean?", I couldn't solve the puzzle.'
'That's simple, Lofty,' Pip replied, 'All it means is muzzle.'

'But I'm a better guard dog,' said Lofty, showing his chip.
'Not for an apartment on Fifth Avenue,' said Pip.
'We live on the nineteenth floor – my owner is a hater
Of great big Giant Schnauzers cluttering up the elevator.'

Lofty was shipped home to his European yard,
Brooding over why his US entry had been barred.
Pip continued breeding, which is why there are today
Miniature Schnauzers everywhere in the USA.

The Afghan Hound

An Afghan is an enormous hound,
So it comes as no surprise
That it rarely tires, and really requires
A great deal of exercise.

If you keep an Afghan cooped up,
I can promise you no sleep.
It'll start to snap, get in a flap,
And then it'll kill some sheep.

Afghans get neurotic
And never bother to think;
A beautiful breed, but what they need,
Is a private Afghan *Shrink*.

So put up a notice for Afghans,
Who are forced to live in town –
'If you're cooped up, since being a pup,
We'll put your owners down'!

Bruce The Australian Kelpie

Bruce the Australian Kelpie
From Queensland's Julia Creek,
Is black and tan, and don't give a damn
About rounding up sheep all week.

Bruce controls about 5000 sheep
With the single glint of his eye.
Any flim-flam from a horny ram,
Is the sort of thing Bruce won't buy.

Everyone knows Bruce the Kelpie,
From Brisbane to Alice Springs.
Each Koala and Roo, and the Abos too,
Plus the sheep who are all ding-a-lings.

So Bruce could expect tremendous respect
From any potential sheep stealer;
And all was OK, until one hot day,
Along came a dingo called Sheila.

She claimed that she was an orphan,
Who was fostered out – what a saga.
She looked like death, Bruce smelt her breath,
And knew that the Foster was lager.

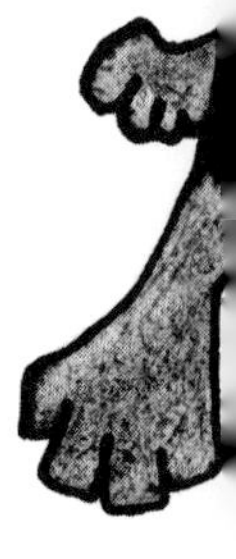

Out of pity he gave her a dog food can,
Which she guzzled down (the glutton)
Then she heaved a sigh, and cast her eye
On those thousands of legs of mutton.

'I don't suppose you got (hic) some mint sauce,'
Slurred Sheila, 'for *Little Bo Peep*?'
Bruce said, 'We'll make camp, and listen, you tramp,
Keep your beady eyes off my sheep.'

Then Sheila crooned 'Waltzing Matilda'
(More howling than crooning in style).
Bruce covered his ears, the Roos shed tears,
And the sheep ran a bloody mile.

When Bruce nodded off, she tip-toed out
All set for a meal of fresh meat;
But her cover was blown, when a lamb on its own
Saw Sheila and let out a bleat.

Bruce sprang awake, and arrived just before
Sheila attacked a lamb chop.
Bruce ripped her coat, and went for her throat,
When a Bruce gets going, he won't stop.

Bruce didn't look, as Sheila
Limped out of sight in shame.
And Aussie men, with a sexy yen,
Behave exactly the same.

If you go to a party in Sydney,
And watch for romantic feelers,
You'll spot each Bruce, looking very spruce,
But *never* going near the Sheilas.

Griffon Bruxellois

The Griffon Bruxellois is mostly red, but can
Turn out very black, or a mix of black and tan.
And for those of you not sure what I'm spouting on about,
The Griffon is a dog and *not* a Brussels sprout!

Prince The Pyrenean Mountain Dog

The Pyrenean Mountain Dog's a breed I hope won't vanish,
Their ancestry is French and never, never Spanish.
As puppies they resemble very cuddly teddy bears,
But they grow to be enormous – have no fears.

A family called Baxter bought a tiny puppy, Prince,
That was three years back, and he's been growing ever since.
Financially the Baxters by now are on the skids
Cause Prince ate even more than all the kids.

The Baxters haven't bought any new clothes for a year –
They can't afford a holiday, not while Prince is there.
Pyrenean Mountain Dogs are certainly worth knowing –
But even as you read this, Prince is growing.

Prince is now so large, he calls himself a king,
As a guard dog and companion, his praises we can sing.
Meanwhile the Baxter family, to warnings have been deaf;
Eventually, I'm afraid, they almost starved to death.

That's the tale of Prince, the Pyrenean Mountain Dog,
And if you found it morbid, your memory I'll jog.
As puppies they resemble very cuddly teddy bears,
But they grow to be enormous – have no fears.

Jack The Manchester Terrier

Jack the Manchester Terrier chases rats a lot,
He catches them and stews them in his Lancashire hot pot.
With ratties down your drain, quickly Jack dispenses,
And all you have to pay are his travelling expenses.

But first a little warning, so do not phone him yet.
Jack will only travel in a private Lear jet.
That's why, down in London, there are lots of rats to meet,
But I'll bet you'll never find one north of Coronation Street!

Reggie The Dandie Dinmont

Reggie the Dandie Dinmont
Has legs that are somewhat bandy;
But he goes everywhere, with such dashing air
That he's known as *Reggie the Dandy*.

He comes from the border counties
Of Dumfries and Galloway –
Then his master, the fool, decided Blackpool
Was ideal for his holiday.

In Blackpool his master stuck on his head
A hat that read *Kiss me Quick*.
Reggie liked the idea, and started to wear
A hat that read *Penny a Lick*.

Soon Reggie was doing tremendous trade,
He was licked all the way down the beach;
Until he espied an ideal *Puppy Bride*,
Very young, but an absolute peach.

First he let her have a good sniff
(Her scent was absolute bliss)
Wasting no time, he said, 'I'm in my prime –
Let me take you away from all this.'

His master was so impressed that he said,
'That's the prettiest puppy I've seen.'
So he drove them by car, but only as far
As the outskirts of Gretna Green.

After they wed in the Kennel Kirk,
They lapped up some lemonade shandy.
The Peach had pups, beautiful pups –
And for Reggie – everything's Dandy!